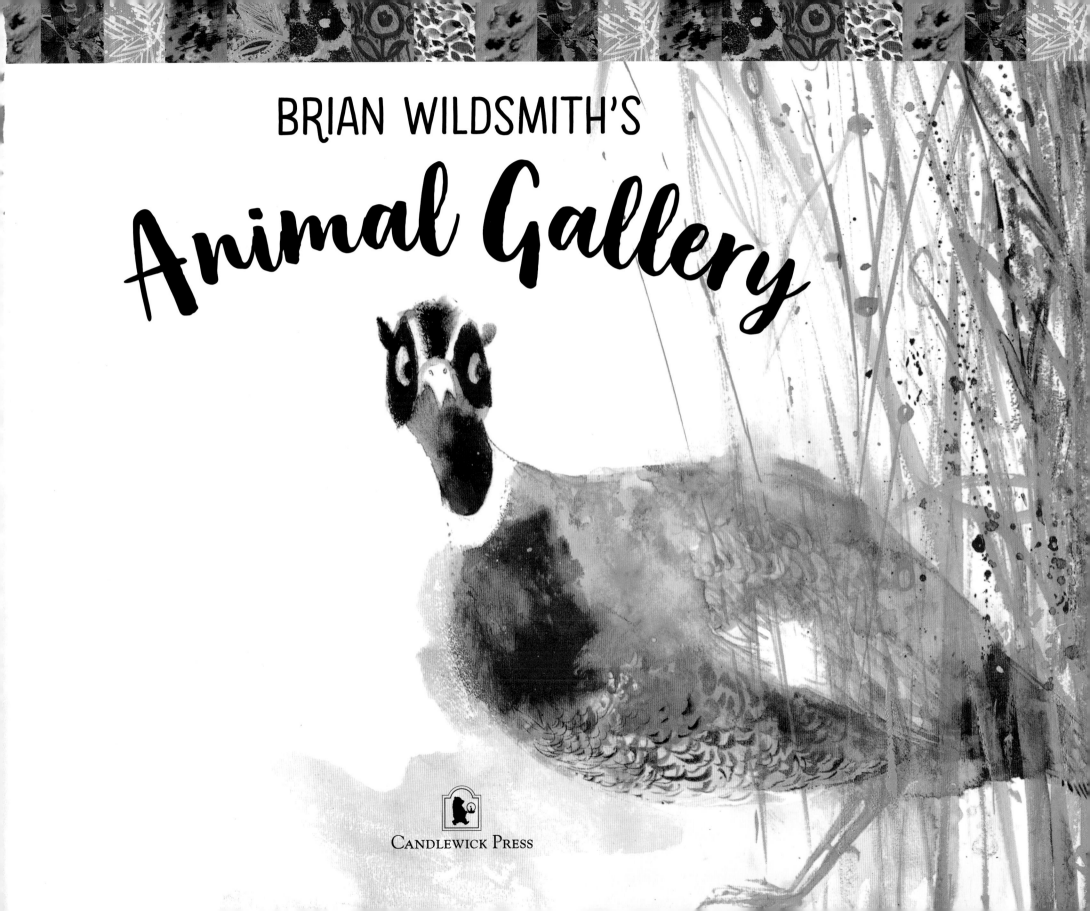

BRIAN WILDSMITH'S
Animal Gallery

CANDLEWICK PRESS

For Simon

First U.S. edition 2020. First published by Oxford University Press (United Kingdom) 2008. Library of Congress Catalog Card Number pending. ISBN 978-1-5362-1235-8. This book was typeset in Amaranth. The illustrations were done in colored pencil and chalk, watercolor, and gouache. Candlewick Studio, an imprint of Candlewick Press, 99 Dover Street, Somerville, Massachusetts 02144. www.candlewickstudio.com. Printed in Heshan, Guangdong, China. 20 21 22 23 24 25 LEO 10 9 8 7 6 5 4 3 2 1

A crash of rhinoceroses

A pride of lions

A shoal
of seahorses

A tower of giraffes

A game of swans

A skulk of foxes

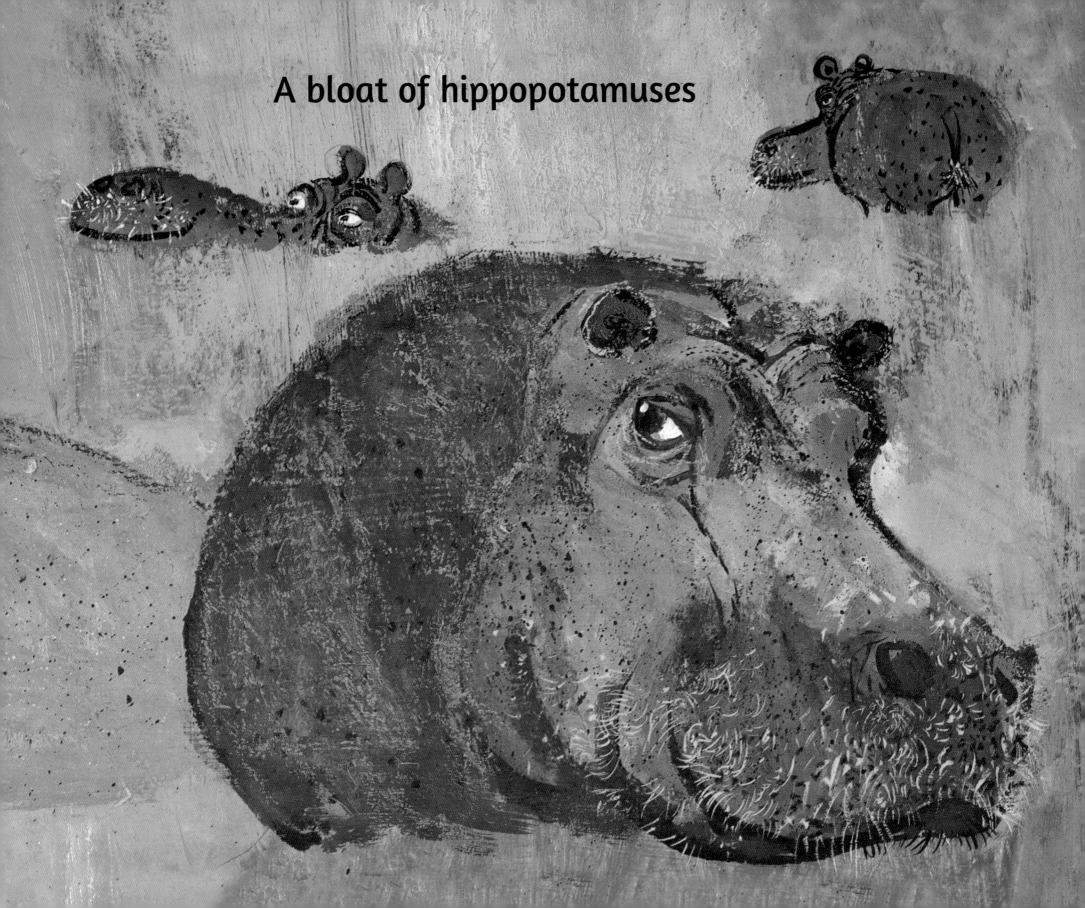

A bloat of hippopotamuses

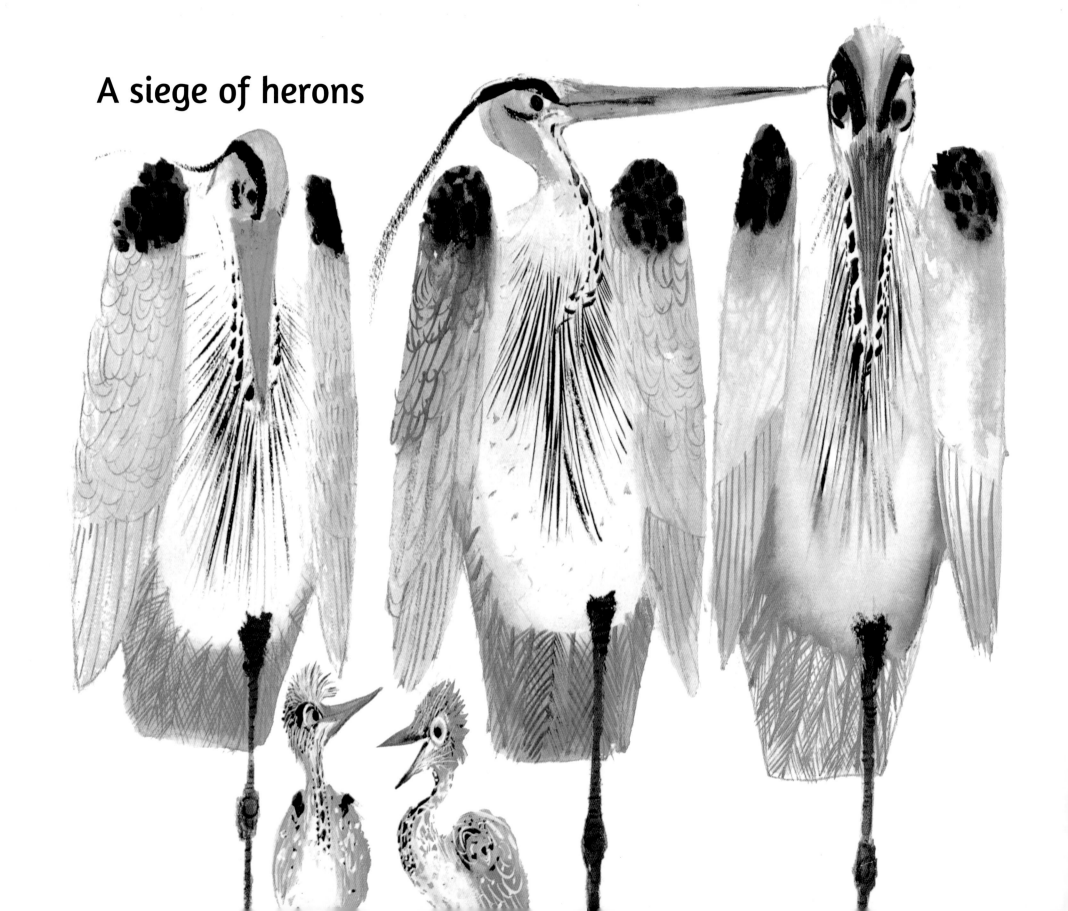

A siege of herons

A flotilla
of swordfish

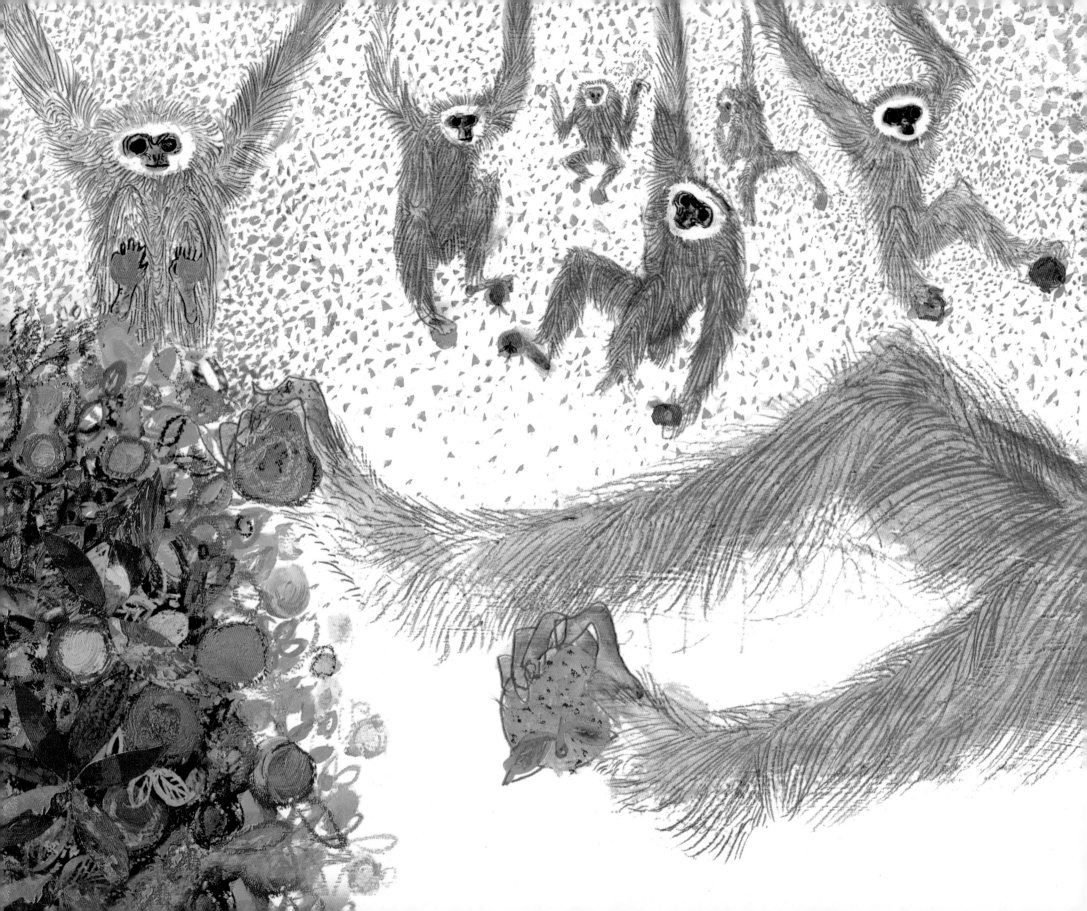

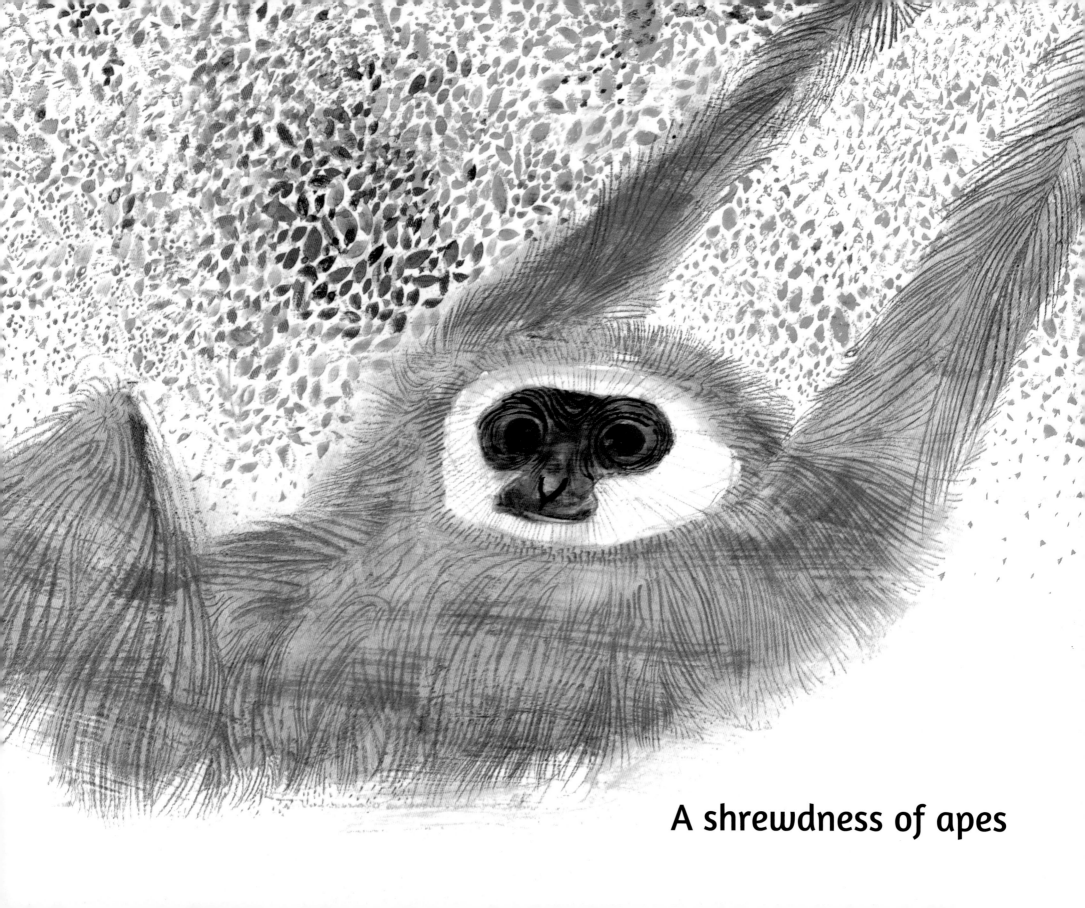

A shrewdness of apes

A troop of kangaroos

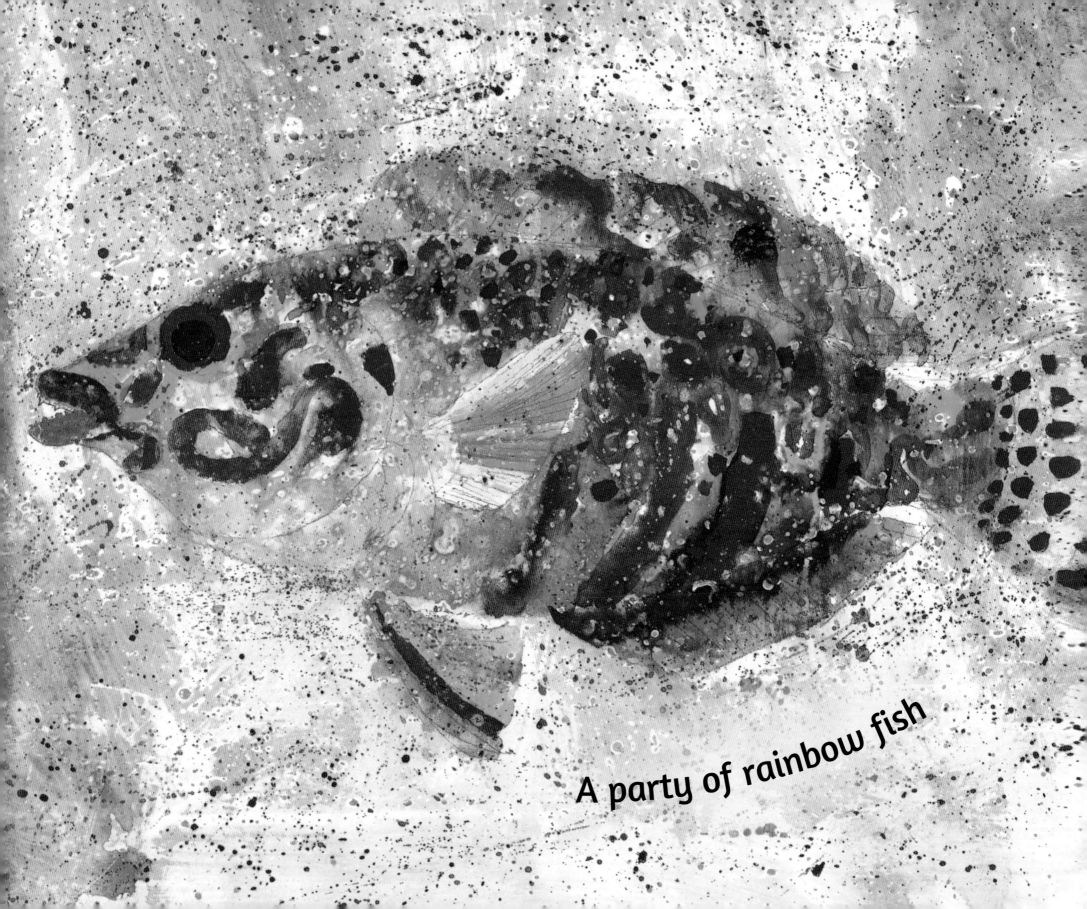

A party of rainbow fish

An ambush
of tigers

A glide of flying fish

A sloth of bears

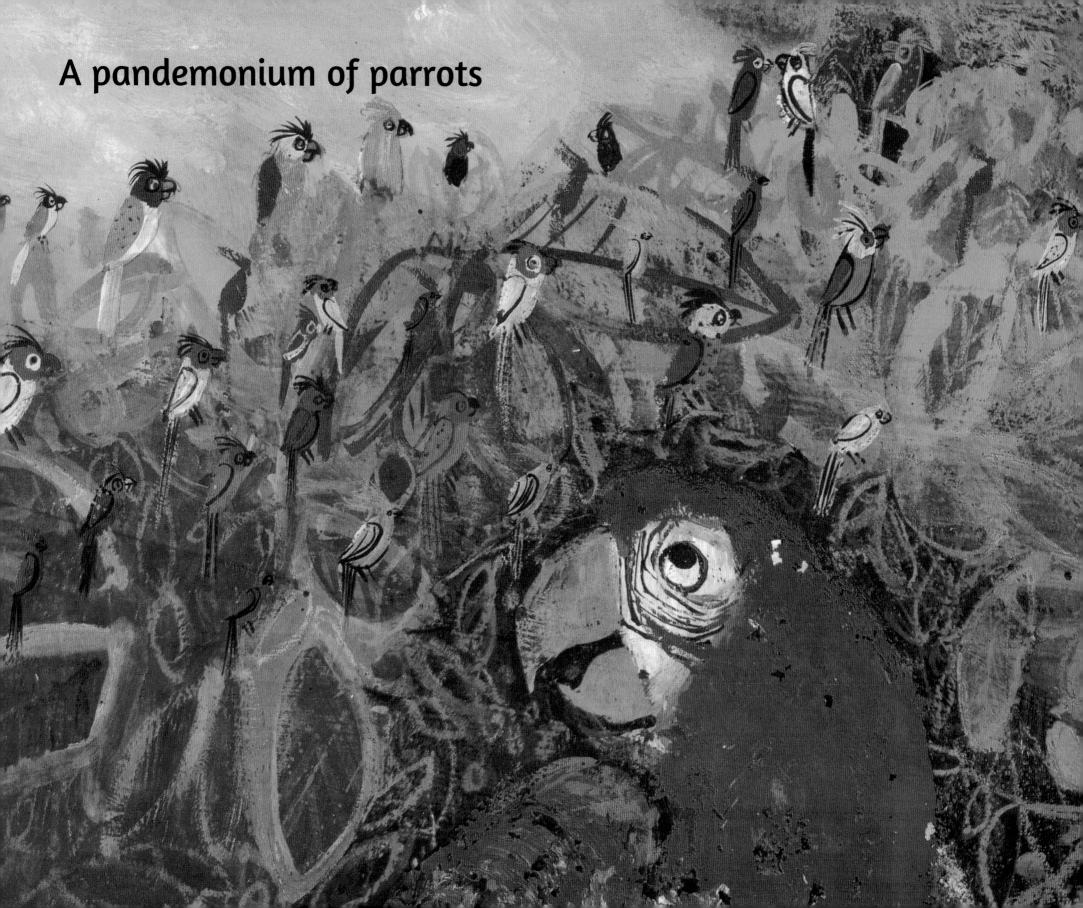

A pandemonium of parrots

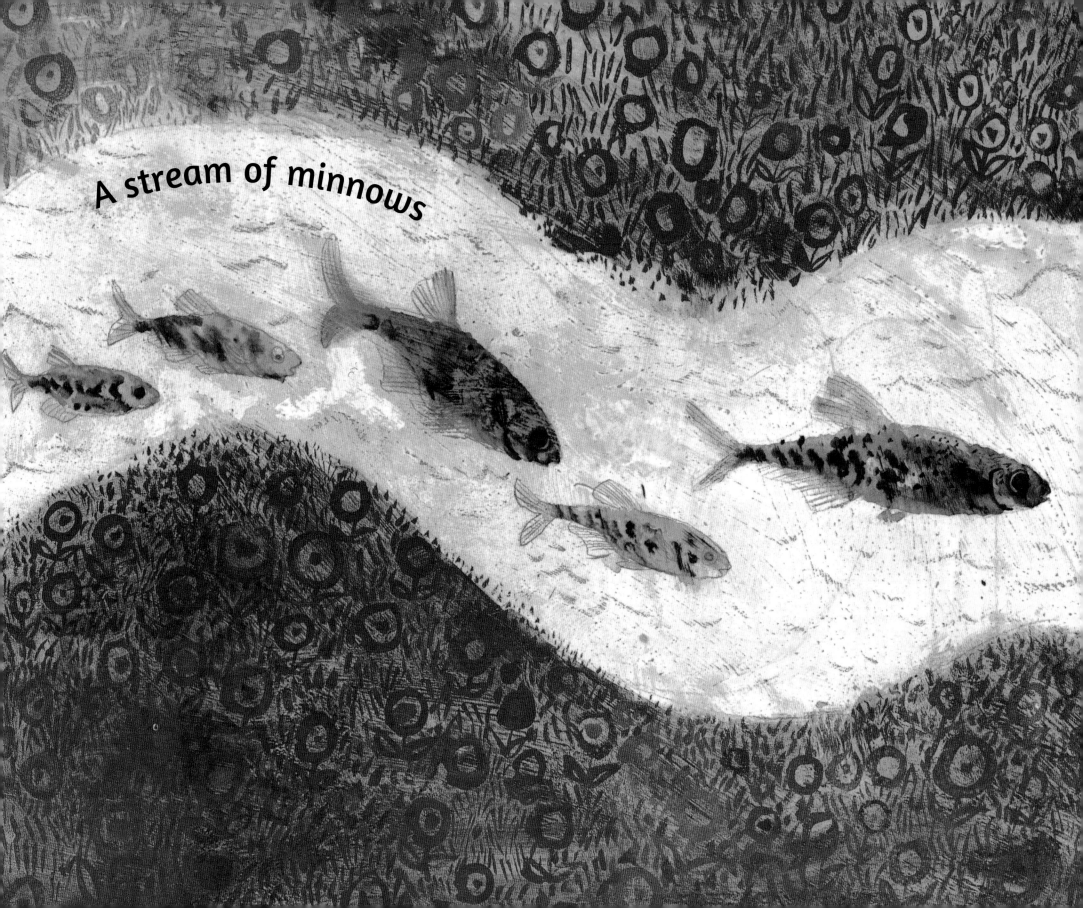

A stream of minnows

A stare of owls

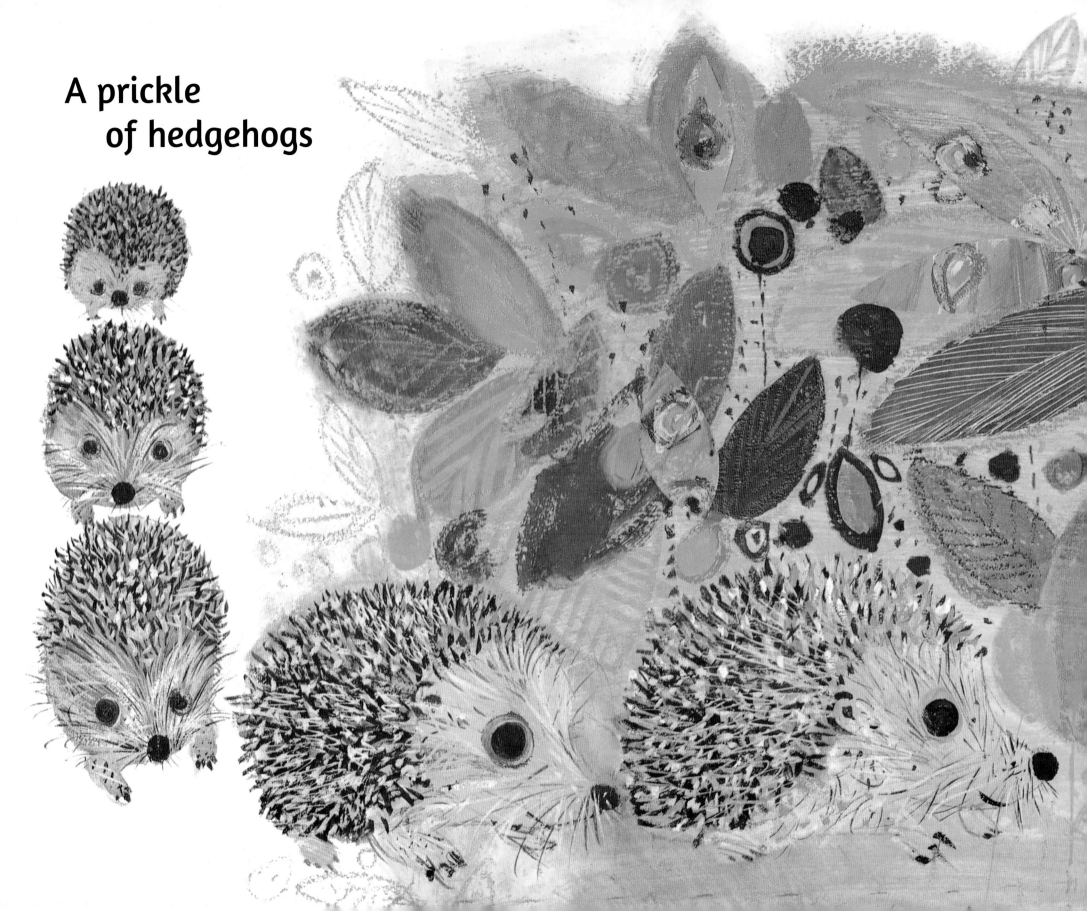

A prickle
of hedgehogs

A family of otters

A hover of trout

A colony of penguins

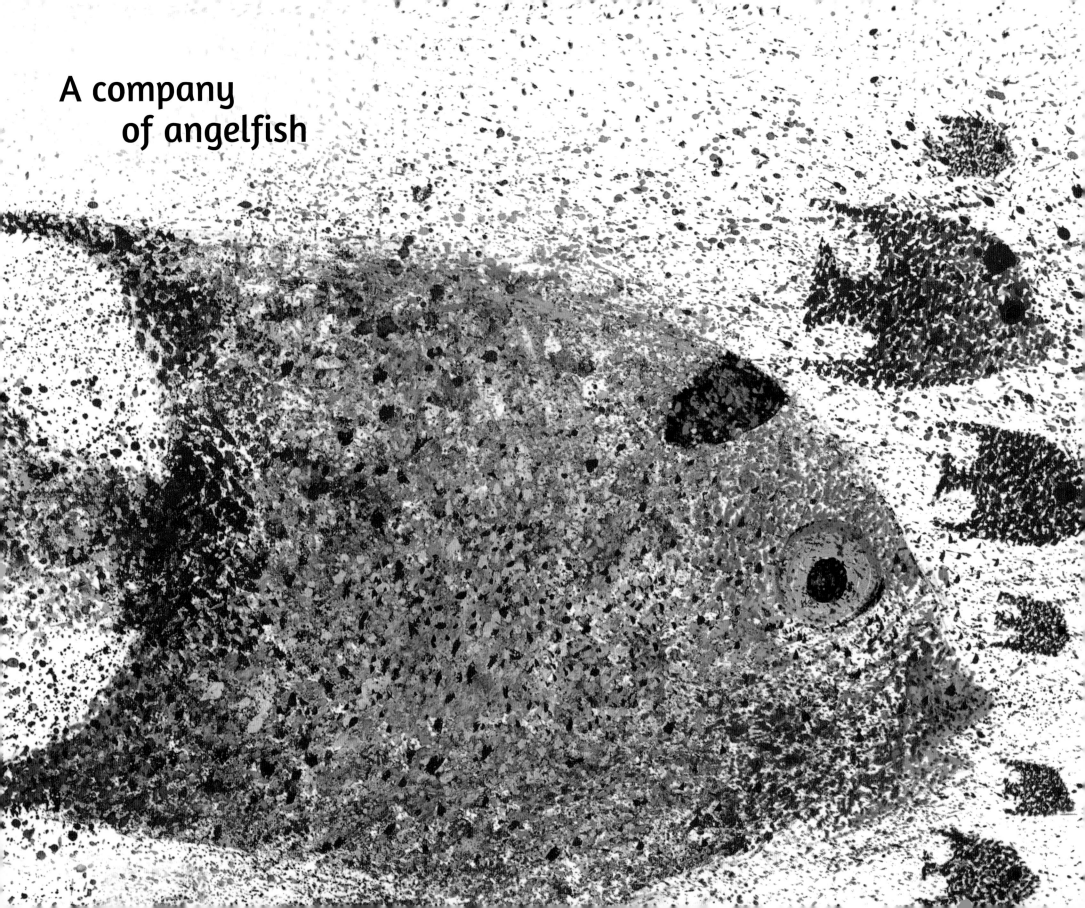

A company
of angelfish

A herd of reindeer

A gaze
of raccoons

A muster of turkeys

A leap of leopards

A parade of elephants

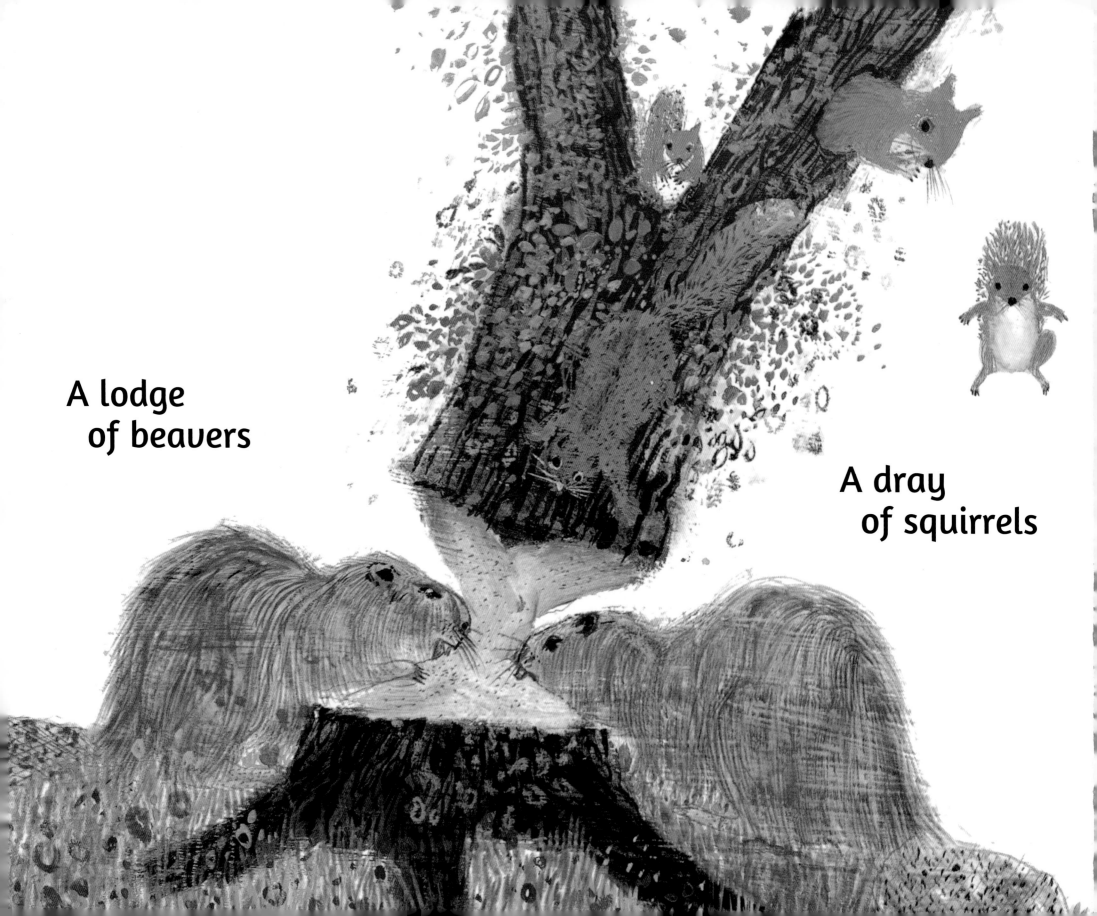

A lodge
of beavers

A dray
of squirrels